D1606931

MEET
BEN
ROETHLISBERGER

Football's Big Ben

PowerKiDS
press™

New York

Published in 2009 by The Rosen Publishing Group, Inc.
29 East 21st Street, New York, NY 10010

First Edition

Editor: Amelie von Zumbusch
Book Design: Greg Tucker
Photo Researcher: Jessica Gerweck

Photo Credits: Cover, pp. 4, 7, 8, 10, 11, 12, 14, 15, 16, 18, 19, 20, 23, 24, 26, 28, 30 © Getty Images; p. 27 © Associated Press.

Library of Congress Cataloging-in-Publication Data

MacRae, Sloan.
    Meet Ben Roethlisberger : football's Big Ben / Sloan MacRae. — 1st ed.
        p. cm. — (All-star players)
    Includes index.
    ISBN 978-1-4358-2706-6 (library binding) — ISBN 978-1-4358-3098-1 (pbk.)
ISBN 978-1-4358-3104-9 (6-pack)
    1. Roethlisberger, Ben, 1982– —Juvenile literature. 2. Football players—United States—Biography—Juvenile literature. I. Title.
    GV939.R64M33 2009
    796.332092—dc22
    [B]
                                                2008021583

Manufactured in the United States of America

Contents

Ben Roethlisberger is 6 feet 5 inches (2 m) tall! However, his skill as a leader is just as important as his height in making him a top quarterback.

Big Ben

Ben Roethlisberger is a great leader. He is a **professional** football player in the National Football League, or NFL. Roethlisberger's nickname is "Big Ben." People call him this because he is so tall. His size makes him hard to tackle.

Roethlisberger is the quarterback for the Pittsburgh Steelers. The quarterback is the leader of a team's **offense**. Quarterbacks need to be good **athletes**, but they also must be smart football players. They must understand **strategy**. Roethlisberger is one of the NFL's top quarterbacks. He has already made NFL history with the Pittsburgh Steelers. In 2006, Roethlisberger became the youngest quarterback ever to win a **Super Bowl**!

Ben Roethlisberger was born in 1982. He grew up in a town called Findlay, Ohio. Roethlisberger's parents divorced when Ben was very young. His father remarried, and Ben spent time with both parents. Sadly, Ben's mother died in a car accident when he was only eight years old.

Even at a young age, Ben was a great athlete. He played football, basketball, and baseball in high school. Football is very important in the area of Ohio where Roethlisberger lived. The sport became very important to Ben, too. Unfortunately, Ben did not get to play quarterback during his first three years of high school. His coach's son was the starting quarterback, so Ben played wide receiver instead.

All-Star Facts

Football was not Roethlisberger's favorite sport as a kid. He preferred playing basketball.

His experience playing wide receiver gave Roethlisberger a better understanding of football and has made him a better quarterback.

Roethlisberger's great playing during his last year of high school convinced coaches at Miami University to recruit him, even though he did not have much experience as a quarterback.

Playing for the RedHawks

By the beginning of his last year of high school, Roethlisberger knew he hoped to go to college on a football **scholarship**. However, he wanted to play quarterback. Unfortunately, the college **recruiters** and coaches knew that Ben had never played that position. In his final year of high school, Ben became the starting quarterback. It did not take Roethlisberger long to prove he was great in that position. He threw six touchdowns in his very first game.

Miami University, in Oxford, Ohio, offered Roethlisberger a scholarship. He played football for the Miami RedHawks. In just three years, Roethlisberger broke nearly all the school's passing records. He was the best quarterback ever to play for Miami University. In his final year, Roethlisberger led the RedHawks to the Mid-American Conference championship. He had

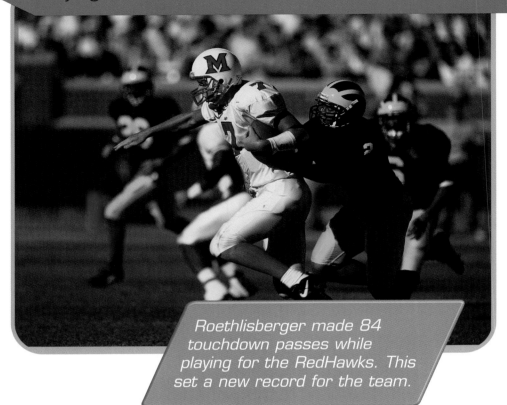

Roethlisberger made 84 touchdown passes while playing for the RedHawks. This set a new record for the team.

achieved the highest goal he could at Miami University. He was ready for the NFL.

Scouts from NFL teams had been watching Big Ben. He was one of the best young quarterbacks in the country. Roethlisberger decided to enter the 2004 NFL Draft. The NFL holds the draft every year. In the draft, teams take turns picking the best young players. There were several excellent quarterbacks in the 2004 draft. The Pittsburgh Steelers picked Ben in the draft's first round. He was about to make football history.

Roethlisberger was picked eleventh out of more than 250 players in the 2004 NFL Draft.

Though the Steelers had not expected Roethlisberger to become a starting quarterback so quickly, he rose to the challenge.

The Pittsburgh Steelers

Steelers coach Bill Cowher did not want Roethlisberger to start in his first NFL season. NFL football is more difficult and more dangerous than college football. The Steelers already had two quarterbacks, named Tommy Maddox and Charlie Batch. Roethlisberger could learn by watching them. Unfortunately, Batch was **injured** in the **preseason**. Maddox was injured in the second game of the regular season. Ready or not, Roethlisberger had to lead his team.

The Steelers did not lose a single regular-season game that Roethlisberger started! They even beat the season's last two undefeated teams, the New England Patriots and the Philadelphia Eagles. No NFL quarterback had ever had a better **rookie** season! Roethlisberger won the Offensive Rookie of the Year Award. The Steelers became the first team in the American Football Conference to win

Along with the NFL Offensive Rookie of the Year Award, Roethlisberger also won the Diet Pepsi NFL Rookie of the Year Award. Fans select the winner of this award.

15 regular-season games. Unfortunately, the Steelers lost to the Patriots in the AFC Championship round of the play-offs.

One of Roethlisberger's best friends on the Steelers was **veteran** running back Jerome Bettis. Bettis was a **mentor** to Roethlisberger. By the end of the 2004 season, Bettis was ready to retire. While he had enjoyed a great NFL career, Bettis had never won a Super Bowl. Roethlisberger begged Bettis to play for one more season. Roethlisberger promised his friend the Steelers would win the Super Bowl the next year.

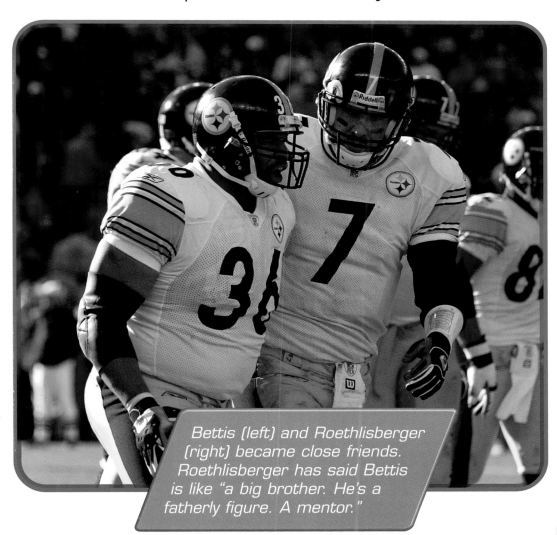

Bettis (left) and Roethlisberger (right) became close friends. Roethlisberger has said Bettis is like "a big brother. He's a fatherly figure. A mentor."

The 2005 season got off to a good start when Roethlisberger and the Steelers beat the Tennessee Titans, 34–7, in the season's first game.

A Promise Kept

Most football **journalists** did not think the Steelers had a chance of winning the Super Bowl. They agreed that the Indianapolis Colts were a much better team. Roethlisberger was injured in the regular season. He missed only a few games, but the Steelers struggled without him. However, Roethlisberger returned in time to help the Steelers reach the play-offs.

The Steelers entered the play-offs with the sixth **seed**. This means they had the worst record of all the teams in the play-offs. No sixth seed had ever reached the Super Bowl. The Steelers would have to win every game on the road in order to reach the Super Bowl. However, home teams usually have an advantage over visiting teams.

Then, the Steelers went on to beat the Cincinnati Bengals, the Indianapolis Colts, and the Denver Broncos. Roethlisberger played well in

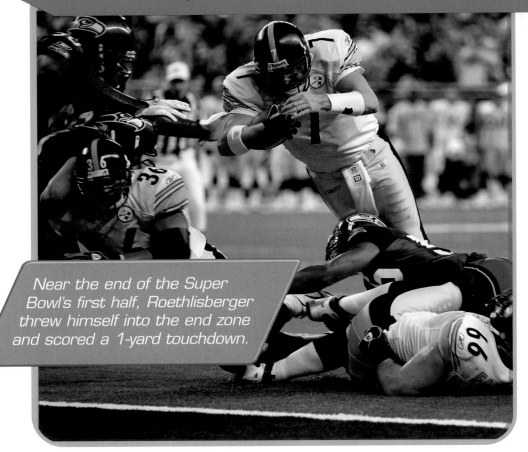

Near the end of the Super Bowl's first half, Roethlisberger threw himself into the end zone and scored a 1-yard touchdown.

each game. He saved the Steelers' season in Indianapolis. Bettis **fumbled** in the final minutes of the game. Colts player Nick Harper picked up the ball. Roethlisberger tackled him. This became one of the most famous plays in Steelers history. Some fans simply call the play "the Tackle."

The Steelers became the first sixth seed to reach the Super Bowl. In the big game, they went on to beat the Seattle Seahawks. Roethlisberger had kept his promise to Bettis.

Coach Bill Cowher (left) and Roethlisberger (right) celebrated their Super Bowl win after the big game on February 5, 2006.

A Bad Year

A few months after the Super Bowl, Roethlisberger almost lost everything. In June 2006, he went for a motorcycle ride through Pittsburgh. He did not wear a helmet. Roethlisberger's motorcycle crashed into a car. He almost died. Roethlisberger's friends and fans feared that he would never play football again. Luckily, Roethlisberger got better. He told his fans that he was sorry and that it was a mistake to ride without a helmet.

To make matters worse, Roethlisberger soon needed an emergency operation to remove his **appendix**. Big Ben did not play well when he stepped back onto the field. Many journalists began to doubt that he would ever play well again.

The 2006 season was a very hard one for Roethlisberger. Fans began to wonder if his days as a top quarterback were over.

Roethlisberger was healthy for the 2007 season. He silenced his doubters by playing some of his best football yet. Roethlisberger threw four touchdowns in the first game of the season. He went on to tie a Steelers record by throwing five touchdowns in a game against the Baltimore Ravens. All five touchdowns came in just the first half of the game.

Ben Roethlisberger led the Steelers into the play-offs once again. Unfortunately, the Steelers lost a close game to the Jacksonville Jaguars. Pittsburgh failed to reach the Super Bowl, but Roethlisberger proved that he was still one of the game's best quarterbacks.

All-Star Facts

Roethlisberger threw 32 touchdown passes during the 2007 regular season. This was a record for a Steelers player.

One of Roethlisberger's most important jobs as a quarterback is to direct the plays of the team's offense.

Roethlisberger's success has made him famous. He now attends awards shows, such as the ESPYs, and is friends with famous people, such as businessman Donald Trump.

Roethlisberger's Roethlis-Burger

Roethlisberger is one of the most famous people in Pittsburgh. There is even a sandwich named after him. Several Pittsburgh restaurants sell the Roethlis-burger. It costs $7 because Roethlisberger wears number seven. Big Ben also sells his own beef jerky and barbecue sauce.

Roethlisberger feels that it is important to help his community. This is why he created the Ben Roethlisberger Foundation. The Ben Roethlisberger Foundation is a charity that raises money for police and fire departments in Pittsburgh and Ohio. In particular, the foundation raises money to train special dogs to work with police, firefighters, and rescue workers. Roethlisberger likes dogs. He has

All-Star Facts

In February 2006, Roethlisberger appeared on the *Late Show with David Letterman*. He shaved his beard while he was on the show!

There are several recipes for the Roethlis-burger. This Roethlis-burger contains beef, sausage, scrambled eggs, onions, and cheese.

a rottweiler, named Zeus, and a Burmese mountain dog, named Hercules.

Roethlisberger has helped people around the world, too. In 2004, a giant **tsunami** killed thousands of people in Indonesia, Sri Lanka, and Thailand. The tsunami also destroyed thousands of homes. Roethlisberger donated, or gave, an entire paycheck to help the **survivors**.

Family is important to Roethlisberger. He loves his father so much that he gave him his Super Bowl ring for Father's Day. Ben still misses his mother. Every time Roethlisberger scores a touchdown, he points to the sky. He hopes that she is looking down on him.

The Roethlisberger family comes from Switzerland. In 2006, Ben Roethlisberger (left) visited Geissbuehl, Lauperswil, the town in which his great-great-grandfather was born.

Always a Steeler

Roethlisberger has accomplished much in a very short time. He won a Super Bowl in just his second season as a professional football player. Most NFL players spend their entire careers trying to win a Super Bowl.

Roethlisberger is just getting started. He is already one of the best quarterbacks in the NFL. He is likely to play for many more seasons. Roethlisberger has said he wants to spend that entire time playing for Pittsburgh. He signed a new contract with the Steelers for $102 million in 2008. This made him one of the richest athletes in the world. The Steelers believe Big Ben is worth every penny.

Roethlisberger is widely believed to be one of today's best young quarterbacks.

Height: 6' 5" (2 m)
Weight: 241 pounds (109 kg)
Team: Pittsburgh Steelers
Position: Quarterback
Uniform Number: 7
Date of Birth: March 2, 1982

2007 Season Stats

Passing Yards	Passing Completions	Passing Touchdowns	Quarterback Rating
3,154	264	32	104.1

Career Stats as of 2007 Season

Passing Yards	Passing Completions	Passing Touchdowns	Quarterback Rating
11,673	908	84	92.5

Glossary

appendix (uh-PEN-diks) A small pouchlike body part that is joined to the gut.

athletes (ATH-leets) People who take part in sports.

fumbled (FUM-buld) Dropped a ball that the other team can pick up.

injured (IN-jurd) Harmed or hurt.

journalists (JER-nul-ists) People who gather and write news for newspapers or magazines.

mentor (MEN-tor) A trusted guide or teacher.

offense (AH-fents) When a team tries to score points in a game.

preseason (PREE-see-zun) A time right before the start of the regular season when players train.

professional (pruh-FESH-nul) Having to do with someone who is paid for what he or she does.

recruiters (rih-KROOT-erz) People who look for new members of a group or team.

rookie (RU-kee) A new major-league player.

scholarship (SKAH-lur-ship) Money given to someone to pay for school.

scouts (SKOWTS) People who help sports teams find new, young players.

seed (SEED) A player or team that has been given a position for a group of play-off games, often at a given level.

strategy (STRA-tuh-jee) Planning and directing different plays in team sports.

Super Bowl (SOO-per BOHL) The championship game of NFL football.

survivors (sur-VY-verz) Things or people that were able to stay alive.

tsunami (soo-NAH-mee) A series of waves caused by a movement in Earth's crust on the ocean floor.

veteran (VEH-tuh-run) A person who has had his or her job for a long time.

Index

Web Sites

Due to the changing nature of Internet links, PowerKids Press has developed an online list of Web sites related to the subject of this book. This site is updated regularly. Please use this link to access the list:
www.powerkidslinks.com/asp/benr/